holiday *Fruit*

holiday *Fruit*

written by

GEORGEANNE BRENNAN


conceived & produced by

JENNIFER BARRY DESIGN


photography by

RICHARD G. JUNG

SMITHMARK

This edition published in 1999 by SMITHMARK Publishers, a division of
U.S. Media Holdings, Inc., 115 West 18th Street, New York, NY 10011.

SMITHMARK books are available for bulk purchase for sales promotion
and premium use. For details, write or call the manager of special sales, SMITHMARK Publishers,
115 West 18th Street, New York, NY 10011.

Conceived and Produced by Jennifer Barry Design, Sausalito, California
Layout Production: Kristen Wurz
Food Stylist: Andrea Lucich
Prop Stylist: Carol Hacker / Tableprop, San Francisco
Craft and Floral Stylist: Sarah Dawson
Copy Editor: Carolyn Miller
Proofreading: Barbara King

Library of Congress Cataloging-in-Publication Data
Brennan, Georgeanne, 1943–
Holiday fruit : a collection of inspired recipes, gifts, and decorations / written by Georgeanne Brennan ;
conceived & produced by Jennifer Barry Design ; photography by Richard Jung.
p.     cm.
Includes index.
ISBN 0-7651-1662-6 (hardcover)
1. Cookery (Fruit)   2. Holiday cookery.   3. Holiday decorations.   I. Title.
TX811.B74     1999
641.6'4--dc21     99-13385     CIP

Printed in Hong Kong

First printing 1999
10 9 8 7 6 5 4 3 2 1

# *Acknowledgments*

Georgeanne Brennan would like to thank the following people:
My husband Jim Schrupp, for his enthusiastic recipe sampling and careful editing.
Robert Wallace for being such a helpful and interested kitchen assistant and recipe tester.
Thanks also to Jennifer Barry for asking me to participate in her Holiday series and allowing
me to be part of yet another of her beautiful books. Carolyn Miller for her diligent editing.
Andrea Lucich for her food styling, and Richard Jung for his photographs.

Jennifer Barry Design and the photography and styling team would like
to thank and acknowledge the following individuals for their help on this book project:
Smithmark editor Gabrielle Pecarsky for her continuing support and enthusiasm
for the Holiday series; Leslie Barry for her beautiful original series design; photography
assistant Ivy for her endless reserve of patience and energy; Tom Johnson for production
assistance; Yankee Girl Antiques, San Anselmo; Nest, San Francisco; and Draeger's, Menlo Park.
Special thanks go to Vicky Kalish and Cecelia Michaelis for their support of this project.

# Introduction

Fruits of all kinds are an important part of holiday foods and festivities. We are fortunate to have a wide variety of fruits available to us throughout the year, even in winter. Fresh fruit comes to us from local producers as well as from exotic climates around the world, while dried fruit, so important in holiday cooking, is always at hand.

Fall-harvested apples, pears, quince, and persimmons are keeper fruits, stored in cool, dry larders and pantries where they can be used throughout the cold season. Oranges, grapefruits, lemons, limes, mandarins, and other citrus fruits ripen during sunny days in the temperate zones of world, such as North Africa, Israel, southern Spain, California, Arizona, and Florida, and are shipped to the colder climates of North America and Europe.

Exotic fruits, once great rarities available only to travelers or people in ethnic enclaves, now come to our markets from the temperate and tropical zones. Mangos, pineapples, and coconuts, made into savories and sweets, are now part of our holiday feasting. Cranberries arrive from the cold bogs of North America in the Pacific Northwest, Cape Cod, and Wisconsin, not far from the Canadian border.

Summer's plentiful fruits, gone from the trees by winter, have been dried, which preserves and intensifies their natural sweetness. Dried apricots, peaches, pears, raisins and even cherries are part of the panoply of the season's stuffings, cookies, pies, salads, and cakes.

Seasonal fruits are as much a part of the holiday scenery as is the holiday feasting. Della Robbia wreaths of citrus, bowls of apples mixed with glistening ornaments, garlands strung with cranberries and pine cones—all decorate tables and doors, reminding us that throughout the year, nature has provided us with a bounty of fruit.

## Apples

Apples can be grown in a wide range of climates, but certain varieties may be suited to one climate and not to another. Among the most popular varieties available nationwide are Red Delicious, Golden Delicious, Granny Smith, Gala, Rome Beauty, McIntosh, and Fuji. At farmers' markets across the country, you can find numerous regional varieties, such as the Arkansas Black, Northern Spy, California's Gravenstein, the Midwest's Empire, and the Baldwin in the East, and many others.

Different apples are best used for different purposes. Generally speaking, for cooking, firm, tart apples that hold their shape are the most desirable. Good choices are Granny Smith, Northern Spy, Golden Delicious, and Rome Beauty, whether to use in pies, to bake, to fry, or to make a chunky sauce. For salads and eating out of hand, sweet apples such as Gala, McIntosh, and the crisp Fuji are better. Some apples, such as Golden Delicious and Pippin are excellent multipurpose apples. All apples can be used to make sauce, but the sauce may be soft and creamy depending on the apple used.

In both sweet and savory uses, apples are complemented by spices such as cinnamon, cloves, and nutmeg. They go well with pork, cabbage, and sausages, and they can be used raw in mixed-fruit salads, green salads, salsas, and gelatin salads, or be served simply with cheeses.

In choosing apples, look for those that are unblemished, smooth, and firm. They should have no soft spots nor any evidence of wrinkling. To keep apples from browning once they have been cut, place them in water that has been acidulated by the addition of lemon juice or vinegar. Or you can just squeeze a little fresh lemon juice over them if it is suitable for the recipe you are using.

## Citrus Fruits: Grapefruits

Grapefruits may be white, red, or pink, with the reds tending to be less acidic than the white varieties. Marsh, which is relatively seedless, is the classic white variety. In recent years, pink and red grapefruits with varietal names such as Ruby and Pink Marsh have become exceedingly popular for their sweet taste and their bright color, especially popular for the holidays in salads, compotes, punches, and for simple fruit drinks.

For salads and compotes, grapefruits are usually peeled and segmented or sliced into rounds. To peel all citrus fruit so that the skin and white pith are removed, try using a sharp knife with a narrow blade, such as a boning knife. Slice off the stem end of the fruit down to the pulp and begin cutting away the skin and pith in a spiral motion around the fruit. When you reach the bottom, cut off the remaining end of the skin.

Segment the fruit by slicing very close to both sides of the membrane dividing each pulp segment. The pulp slices should fall out easily. Be sure to save and squeeze out the wonderful juice left in the segmented fruit shell. The leftover zest is useful for flavoring and the peel can be candied and sugared.

When choosing grapefruits, pick them up. They should feel heavy for their size. If a grapefruit feels somewhat light, there is a good chance it will be mealy and dry inside. Store grapefruit in a cool, dry place.

## Lemons and Limes

Although there are a number of varieties of lemons, we usually see only two or three different ones in our markets, the Eureka and Lisbon, with the Meyer being a specialty variety. Culinarily, the Eureka and Lisbon are essentially interchangeable, but the Meyer lemon is much sweeter and it has a much thinner skin.

The two most common lime varieties are the small, yellow-green Mexican lime, which is grown in Mexico and Florida, and the slightly larger, yellowish Bearss lime, which is closely related to, if not the same as, the Persian or Tahiti lime, and grown in California. The Key lime is the same as the Mexican lime but is named after the specific area where it grows, the Florida Keys. The small, orange Rangpur lime, which is actually a member of the mandarin family, is grouped with limes because of its sour flavor and small size.

Limes, like lemons, have a sour taste, but they are nevertheless slightly sweeter than lemons. Their juice and zest can be used in drinks, salads, and savory dishes, and they are especially good with fish and tropical fruits.

Lemons and limes are very versatile fruits. Their juice and zest are used as primary ingredients in pies, cakes, and cookies, but when other fruits are the primary ingredient, lemons and limes also play important roles in flavoring. Apple pies, pear compotes and tarts, and melons all rely on lemon to bring out and enhance their flavors. Zest and a hint of juice add a sprightly flavor to both hot and cold drinks, ranging from martinis to hot mulled wine, and a twist of zest serves as a classic garnish for numerous drinks. Even candied peel is important, especially in holiday baking, contributing its sweet flavor to fruitcakes and cookies. Lemon and lime juice can be used for salad dressings, to deglaze pans, to squeeze over vegetables and fish, and to make ices and puddings.

In choosing lemons and limes, gently scratch or rub the rind. Fresh, ripe fruit will release an intensely sweet aroma. The fruit should feel heavy for its size, and there should not be a tear at the stem end where the fruit was picked.

## Oranges and Mandarins

In northern Europe, oranges and mandarins have long been a symbol of Christmas because the juicy, exotic fruit from the Mediterranean climes were a treasured, special treat.

Like lemons, oranges are used as both a primary ingredient and a flavoring element. But unlike the lemon, the meat of the sweet orange can be segmented or sliced and used in salads, compotes, and cooked dishes. Oranges go especially well with salty flavors such as feta cheese, black olives, anchovies, and smoked salmon. They also combine well with other fruits, as well as with chicken, pork, and beef.

Freshly squeezed orange juice is a refreshing seasonal drink on its own, but combined with Champagne it becomes an elegant apéritif for any holiday occasion. It can also be mixed with other citrus juices.

The navel is the classic orange of winter. Easy to peel, seedless, large, and very sweet, it is an all-purpose orange. The Valencia orange ripens later in the year and is not typically available in winter. Blood oranges, however, ripen in winter and have a sweet, berry-flavored juice, often a deep garnet red with skin to match. The bitter Seville oranges, though not easy to find, are the classic orange to use for marmalade.

Mandarins, also called tangerines, are considerably smaller than oranges, with a peel that easily detaches from the fruit. With a more delicate, sweeter flavor than oranges, they are excellent in salads and are used to make ices or compotes.

Choose oranges and mandarins as you do grapefruit, judging them by their size and their weight in your hand. Fruits that feel light for their size indicate scant juice and will be dry and pithy. Store oranges and mandarins in a cool, dry place or refrigerator.

## Cranberries

Cranberries are a seasonal specialty, harvested in October in time for holiday tables. They are native to North America and are cultivated only in the United States and Canada, where they are grown in bogs or swampy land that is flooded at harvesttime. They were once harvested by hand, but today cranberries are harvested by machines that "beat" the berries from their low-growing vines. The berries then float to the surface, where they are scooped up and taken for processing.

Cranberries are extremely tart and are usually cooked with sugar before eating. A classic use of cranberries is in cranberry sauce, an essential dish on American holiday tables, but they can be used in a variety of other ways, such as in breads, cakes, pies, cookies, chutneys, and salads.

Frozen cranberries can be substituted for fresh in virtually any prepared dish. Unless otherwise directed, they should be used thawed. Dried cranberries are also available, and while still tart, they are sweeter than fresh cranberries because their natural sugars have been concentrated. They are especially good for baking.

In the kitchen, cranberries have an affinity for apples, pears, oranges, celery, nuts, turkey, chicken, game, and pork. When choosing fresh cranberries, make sure the berries are firm and unbruised. Once purchased, store them in the refrigerator, where they will keep for several weeks. If fresh cranberries are frozen, they can be kept for up to six months.

## Mangos

Fall through late winter is the peak season for mangos, a tropical fruit that grows in the East Indies, Malaysia, Mexico, California, and Florida, as well as in other tropical and semitropical regions. Although there are many different varieties in a range of colors and sizes, the most commonly found are those with sweet, deep orange to yellow flesh, weighing about one-third to one-half pound each. Larger ones, weighing up to three or four pounds, are sometimes available as well.

Culinarily, the mango is wonderfully versatile, as it serves equally well as a sweet for dessert preparations and as a savory to accompany meats, fish, and shellfish, and to use in salads of all kinds.

Mangos have a large center seed that is approximately one-third the size of the fruit and is the same shape as the mango, with flattened sides. To peel and seed the fruit, peel with a paring knife or vegetable peeler, then stand the mango upright on its end and slice downward along the flat side of the seed to remove one large oval of pulp. Repeat along the other side of the seed, and slice the large ovals into segments or chunks.

In choosing mangos, look for those that are firm and unwrinkled, with a fine golden-red blush on the skin. They should be unblemished. Store them at room temperature, where they will keep for several days.

## Pears

Pears, like apples and quince, are harvested in late summer and fall, and certain good storage varieties are kept throughout the winter, making them one of the holiday season's major fruits. Red Bartlett, Anjou, and Bosc are among the winter pears available.

Most varieties of pears can be used interchangeably, but when you want pears to hold their shape during cooking, in a compote or tart for example, choose firm ones. If you want a softer fruit for a sauce or a salad but have only firm pears, leave them out at room temperature for several days to ripen.

Pears can be used in both sweet and savory ways, and find especially good flavor accompaniments with limes, fish, chocolate, vanilla, brown sugar, wines, and Cognac. Pears are also excellent poached in a simple sugar syrup flavored perhaps with vanilla and lemon, or in a wine-based syrup.

When choosing pears, consider how soon you want to use them. A soft pear should be used immediately, but firmer pears will keep for several days. Avoid pears that have brown spots, scarring, or soft spots. Store pears in a cool, dry place or at room temperature to ripen.

## Persimmons

Persimmons, with their deep, bright orange color, make an excellent addition to the holiday table. They are available for only a few months in the fall, usually from October through December. There are two main varieties, each with its different characteristics.

The heart-shaped, pointed Hachiya persimmon must become very, very soft before its sweet flavor is fully developed and the acidic bite of the underripe fruit is completely absent. When fully ripe, the fruit is a deep, burnished reddish color. Fuyu, the other main variety, is a flattened globe and will still be firm when ripe. Because of their differences in texture, the pulpy Hachiya is used for mixing into baked goods, and the crisp, firm Fuyu is ideal for salads and chutneys.

In baking, persimmons go well with brown sugar, toasted nuts, lemons, oranges, and raisins. In savory dishes, limes, cilantro, sesame seeds, cabbage, and other fruits are good choices.

When choosing Hachiya persimmons, avoid those that are quite firm, or allow a week to ten days for them to ripen to edible softness. Choose those that are very soft, even slightly wrinkled, for immediate use. Select Fuyus that have a deep orange color, but are still firm and unwrinkled, or allow several days for ripening if the skin is bright but not deep orange. Avoid any fruit with scarring or hard, dark spots. Store persimmons in a cool, dry location or at room temperature to ripen.

## Quinces

Quince is an old-fashioned fruit that is regaining some of its popularity. It has an intense aroma and an unusual flavor. Unlike other fruits, quince is inedible when raw and must first be cooked. Once cooked, its white flesh sometimes turns a rosy amber and becomes the consistency of a firm, cooked apple, but with a slightly citrusy flavor.

Quinces make wonderful pies and tarts, but they can also be sautéed, fried, or stuffed with a savory filling. They can be marinated before cooking, or simmered in a simple sugar- or wine-based syrup to make a compote. Pork and quince have a particular affinity for one another in savory dishes, and when used in sweets, cinnamon, star anise, nutmeg, and lemon all bring out its flavor.

Choose quinces that are yellow, not green, and that have a distinct and fragrant aroma. Any bruise will rapidly spread decay, so be sure to avoid bruised or scarred fruit. Store quinces in a cool, dry place or at room temperature for up to one week.

Quinces can also be ripened at room temperature and will fill your home with their lovely delicate aroma.

## Raspberries

Raspberries are grown in the northern climates and are typically harvested twice a year in early and late summer. However, they also grow in greenhouses and in the Southern Hemisphere, making them available for the winter season, where their color and sharply sweet flavor contribute to the holiday table. Frozen raspberries, which are excellent for purées, can also be used if you can't find fresh ones. There are three main types of raspberries—black, yellow, and red—and the red is the most commonly available.

All raspberries make superb sauces for both sweet and savory dishes. They can be used in salads, to make desserts, and to garnish desserts and drinks. A few of the foods that raspberries are amenable to are chocolate, pears, pork, game birds, mint, melon, and basil. In choosing raspberries, the main consideration is to pick those that show absolutely no signs of molding. Raspberries can be stored for several days in the refrigerator, but are best used within a day or two of purchase.

## Dried Fruits

A wide range of dried fruits is available, from the humble raisin to the exotic mango, with apricots, cherries, peaches, nectarines, plums, and pineapple included. Dried fruits have intensely concentrated flavors, and a relatively small amount will add great depth to baked goods, sauces, roasts, glazes, and stews. They are essential ingredients for holiday fruitcakes and plum puddings, cookies, cakes, and savory stuffings. Pork roast cooked with dried apricots, corn bread stuffing with dried cherries and currants for poultry, or ham with a dried cherry glaze are all dishes worthy of a holiday meal centerpiece.

Dried fruit can be difficult to cut, and kitchen scissors are often easier to use for the task than a knife. Depending upon the specific preparation, the fruit may be used in its dried state or rehydrated in a little warm water.

When choosing dried fruit, look for fruit that is supple and leathery, not stiff or hard. Store dried fruit in plastic bags in a cool, dry place or in the freezer, where it will keep for up to six months.

# preserves & salads

2

# Winter Pear and Walnut Chutney

THIS SPICY CONDIMENT IS A GOOD ACCOMPANIMENT TO PORK, CHICKEN, AND TURKEY DISHES AS WELL AS TO CURRIES.

IT IS ALSO TASTY WITH DARK BREAD AND CHEDDAR CHEESE.

5 to 6 firm winter pears such as
Winter Nellis, Bosc, or Red Bartlett, peeled,
cored, and diced (3-1/2 to 4 cups)

1 tablespoon fresh lemon juice

2 cups firmly packed brown sugar

1 cup cider vinegar

1/2 cup finely chopped onion

1 tablespoon minced lemon zest

1 cinnamon stick, about 4 inches long

1-inch piece fresh gingerroot, peeled and minced

1 cup raisins

1/4 teaspoon salt

1 cup coarsely chopped walnuts

In a large bowl, combine the pears with the lemon juice and stir to mix them.

In a large stainless steel or other nonreactive saucepan, combine the sugar, vinegar, onion, and lemon zest. Cook over low heat, stirring, until the sugar dissolves, 5 to 6 minutes. Add the pears, cinnamon stick, and gingerroot. Increase heat to medium and cook, stirring often, until the pears are soft and beginning to dissolve, about 30 minutes. Add the raisins, salt, and walnuts. Cook another 15 minutes, stirring often.

Ladle the chutney into dry, sterilized jars, close with the lids, and store in the refrigerator for up to 3 weeks. To keep longer, process in a hot water bath for 30 minutes (see instructions on page 19). Store in a cool, dark place for up to 1 year. Refrigerate after opening. *Makes about 2 pints*

# Hot Water Processing

Wash and rinse canning jars and two-part vacuum lids. Sterilize the jars by submerging them in boiling water for 10 minutes. Submerge the two-part lids in a pan of water and bring almost to a boil. Remove from heat. Using a jar lifter or tongs, transfer the jars to a wire rack or cloth to drain upside down.

Fill the jars to within 1/2 inch of the rim. Wipe the rims clean. Using tongs, remove a lid from the water and place it on the jar. Using tongs, remove a ring from the water and place it on the jar. Using a thick, dry cloth, screw the ring closed fairly tightly. Using long-handled tongs or a jar holder, lower the jars into a canning kettle or other large pot of boiling water fitted with a rack, making sure the jars are not touching. If necessary, add additional water to cover the jar tops with at least 1/2 inch of water. Cover the pot and process in the boiling water according to the recipe. Remove the jars and let cool at room temperature for 12 hours or overnight. Check the seal: The center of each lid should be slightly concave. If not, push down on the lid. If it does not stay down, store the contents in the refrigerator for up to 3 weeks. Store sealed jars in a cool, dark place for up to 1 year.

# Chunky Cinnamon Applesauce

THE TRICK TO A CHUNKY APPLESAUCE IS CHOOSING APPLES THAT HOLD THEIR SHAPE DURING COOKING, SUCH AS GRANNY SMITHS, NORTHERN SPIES, OR BALDWINS. FRESHLY GROUND CINNAMON ADDS A VIBRANT, SPICY TASTE. IT CAN BE MILLED IN A SPICE GRINDER OR A COFFEE MILL.

1 cup granulated sugar

1 cup water

2 pounds tart apples, peeled, cored, and cut into 1/2-inch dice

1/2 teaspoon freshly ground cinnamon

In a large saucepan, combine the sugar and water. Bring to a boil over high heat, stirring to dissolve the sugar, about 5 minutes. Add the apples, cover tightly, and reduce heat to medium-low. Continue to cook, stirring occasionally, until the apples have softened and are translucent, about 25 minutes. Using a handheld beater or a potato masher, mash a few of the apples, leaving the majority chunky. Stir in the cinnamon. Serve hot, warm, at room temperature, or chilled. *Makes 5 to 6 cups*

# Cranberry, Dried Cherry, and Almond Conserve

SINCE CRANBERRIES ARE SUCH AN IMPORTANT ELEMENT OF THE WINTER HOLIDAY SEASON,

IT IS FUN TO HAVE SEVERAL DIFFERENT PREPARATIONS OF THEM FOR THE HOLIDAY TABLE. JARS OF THIS CONSERVE

ALSO MAKE A COLORFUL, HOMEY GIFT FOR A FRIEND OR NEIGHBOR.

3 cups (12 ounces) fresh or frozen cranberries

1-1/2 cups water

3/4 cup honey

3 tablespoons fresh lemon juice

2 star anise pods

2-inch piece of fresh gingerroot, peeled and minced

1/2 cup dried cherries

1/2 cup dried cranberries

2/3 cup coarsely chopped almonds

In a medium saucepan, combine the cranberries, water, honey, lemon juice, star anise, and gingerroot. Bring to a boil over medium-high heat. Reduce heat to low and simmer, uncovered, for 5 minutes. Add the dried cherries and cranberries and simmer another 5 minutes, stirring occasionally. Remove the star anise and discard. Remove from heat and stir in the almonds.

Ladle the hot conserve into hot, sterilized canning jars to within 1/2 inch of the rim and seal. Let cool and refrigerate for up to 3 weeks. For longer storage, seal with two-part lids and process in a hot-water bath (see instructions on page 19). *Makes 4 half-pints*

# Mango-Orange Jam

ORANGE JUICE AND ORANGE ZEST ADD A WONDERFUL TANG TO THIS DELICATE TROPICAL WINTER FRUIT JAM. VALENCIA

OR NAVEL ORANGES WILL MAKE A SWEETER JAM, WHILE SEVILLE, OR BITTER, ORANGES WILL ADD A SLIGHTLY TARTER NOTE.

IT MAKES AN EXCELLENT CONDIMENT TO SERVE WITH A HOLIDAY HAM, OR IF SPREAD OVER CREAM CHEESE AND CRACKERS

AND SPRINKLED WITH ALMONDS, AN UNUSUAL APPETIZER. FOR DESSERT, SPOON IT OVER ICE CREAM OR POUND CAKE.

3 pounds ripe mangos, peeled, cut from the pit,
and coarsely chopped

1 teaspoon fresh lemon juice

1/4 cup fresh orange juice, strained

2 tablespoons finely grated orange zest

1/2 packet (1 ounce) powdered pectin
(2 tablespoons)

3 cups granulated sugar

22

In a 3-quart pan, combine the mangos, lemon juice, orange juice, orange zest, and pectin. Mash well with a potato masher until well mixed. Place over high heat and bring to a rolling boil, stirring. When you are unable to stir the boil down, gradually pour in the sugar, stirring. Return to a rolling boil and cook for exactly 2 minutes, stirring occasionally. Remove, ladle into hot, sterilized jars to within 1/2 inch of the rim, and seal. Store in the refrigerator for up to 6 months. For longer storage, seal with two-part lids and process in a hot-water bath (see instructions on page 19). *Makes 3 half-pints*

# Citrus Marmalade

CITRUS MARMALADES ARE ONE OF THE MOST BEAUTIFUL OF PRESERVES. IN MARMALADE, THE RINDS OF THE FRUIT AS WELL AS THE PULP ARE INCLUDED. FIRST, THE RINDS ARE COOKED UNTIL THEY ARE SOFT, WHICH TAKES VARYING AMOUNTS OF TIME FOR DIFFERENT CITRUS. ORANGES REQUIRE ABOUT 1 HOUR, LEMONS 30 MINUTES (15 MINUTES FOR THE THIN-SKINNED MEYER LEMONS), AND LIMES ABOUT 15 MINUTES.

4 pounds lemons, oranges, or limes

2 to 3 cups water

1 box (2 ounces) powdered pectin

9-1/2 cups granulated sugar

Trim the ends from the lemons, then slice them very thinly into rounds. Remove the seeds. In a stainless steel or other non-reactive pan, combine the lemons and water. Bring to a boil over medium-high heat, then reduce heat to low and simmer, uncovered, for 30 minutes (adjust time as directed above if using limes or oranges), or until the rinds are soft, stirring occasionally. Measure the fruit and liquid to make 7 cups. If necessary, add a little more water.

Return to the saucepan and thoroughly stir in the pectin. Increase heat to medium-high and bring to a boil. Boil for 1 minute, then stir in the sugar and boil 4 minutes longer. Remove from heat and let sit for several minutes, stirring frequently to distribute the peels evenly.

Skim any foam from the surface and ladle the hot marmalade into hot, sterilized canning jars to within 1/2 inch of the rim. Seal tightly and turn the jars upside down several times to distribute the peels. Store in the refrigerator for up to 6 months. For longer storage, seal with two-part vacuum lids and process in a hot-water bath (see instructions on page 19). *Makes 11 half-pints*

# Rosemary-Lemon Oil

OLIVE OIL, INFUSED WITH THE FLAVOR OF ROSEMARY AND LEMON, MAKES A FINE BASTING OIL FOR GRILLING.

IT CAN ALSO BE DRIZZLED ONTO GRILLED BREAD, ITALIAN STYLE, TOSSED WITH PASTA, AND USED FOR MAKING VINAIGRETTES.

THIS MAKES AN ESPECIALLY GOOD VINAIGRETTE FOR POTATO, BEET, AND OTHER VEGETABLE SALADS.

2 cups extra virgin olive oil

Six 6-inch-long fresh rosemary sprigs

1 lemon, quartered

In a glass jar with a lid, combine the olive oil, rosemary, and lemon. Put in a warm, dark place for 1 week. Taste. When the oil is flavored to your liking, strain the oil through a sieve lined with several layers of cheesecloth. Discard the rosemary and the lemon. Funnel into a bottle and seal. Store in a cool, dark place, where it will keep for 6 months. *Makes about 2 cups*

# Citrus and Scallop Salad

TANGY ORANGES AND GRAPEFRUITS MAKE A COMPLEMENTARY BACKGROUND FOR WARM, CARAMELIZED SCALLOPS,

ALL SERVED ON A BED OF FRISÉE AND LIGHTLY DRESSED WITH A LEMON VINAIGRETTE.

1 orange

1/2 grapefruit

4 cups ivory to light green frisée leaves
from the inner heart

1/4 cup fresh lemon juice (about 2 lemons)

1 shallot, minced

3 tablespoons extra virgin olive oil

1 teaspoon salt

1/2 teaspoon freshly ground black pepper

8 sea scallops, halved horizontally

2 tablespoons orange juice mixed with
2 tablespoons fresh lemon juice

With a knife, peel and segment the orange and grapefruit. Cut the orange sections into halves and the grapefruit sections into thirds, discarding any seeds. Put the fruit in a large bowl. Tear the frisée leaves into bite-sized pieces and add them to the bowl. In a small bowl, combine the lemon juice, shallot, olive oil, 1/2 teaspoon of the salt, and the pepper and mix with a fork. Pour this over the fruit and frisée, tossing to coat. Divide the salad equally among 4 salad plates and set aside.

Pat the scallops dry. In a skillet just large enough to hold the scallops, heat the remaining 1/2 teaspoon salt over high heat for about 1 minute. Add the scallops and cook them for about 30 seconds, or until lightly browned. Turn them and cook another 30 seconds, or until lightly browned. Add the orange juice mixture. Cover the pan, reduce heat to low and cook for about 1 minute, or until the scallops are opaque throughout. (Overcooking will toughen the scallops.)

Remove from heat, and using a slotted spoon, place 4 pieces of scallop atop each salad plate. Pour a little of the pan juices over each. Serve immediately. *Serves 4*

# Compote of Red and White Grapefruit with Cointreau

GRAPEFRUITS ARE ONE OF THE CLASSIC FRUITS OF WINTER. WHEN GENTLY POACHED IN
A SYRUP AND FLAVORED WITH A LITTLE COINTREAU, THEY CAN BE A REFRESHING AND UNUSUAL BEGINNING
TO A HOLIDAY MEAL. IF YOU PREFER A BREAKFAST VERSION, SIMPLY OMIT THE COINTREAU.

2 red grapefruits

1 white grapefruit

1-1/2 cups water

1/2 cup granulated sugar

2 tablespoons Cointreau

4 sprigs of mint

Peel and segment the grapefruits with a knife. Remove the seeds and the white pith. In a saucepan, combine the water, sugar, and about half the peel from one of the red grapefruits. Bring to a boil over medium-high heat, stirring to dissolve the sugar. Add the grapefruit, reduce heat to low and simmer for 25 minutes, or until the segments have softened but still hold their shape.

Remove from heat and discard the peel. Stir in the Cointreau, then let the grapefruit segments cool to room temperature in their syrup. Cover and refrigerate for 24 hours. Garnish with a mint sprig before serving. *Serves 5 to 6*

# Blood Orange, Anchovy, and Olive Salad

IN THIS INTRIGUING, FIRST-COURSE NORTH AFRICAN SALAD, THE SWEET, SLIGHTLY
BERRY-FLAVORED BLOOD ORANGES MARRY WELL WITH THE SALTY TASTE OF THE ANCHOVIES AND
THE OLIVES. VALENCIA OR NAVEL ORANGES COULD BE USED AS WELL.

4 blood oranges

4 to 6 anchovy fillets

10 to 12 salt-cured black olives or brined green olives

2 tablespoons extra virgin olive oil

Using a large knife, cut off the rind from the top, bottom, and
sides of the oranges. Thinly slice the oranges. Arrange the
orange rounds attractively on a serving dish. Lay the anchovy
fillets and olives on top, and then drizzle all with the olive oil.
Cover with plastic wrap and refrigerate for 5 to 6 hours or
overnight, allowing the flavors to blend. Remove from the
refrigerator about 30 minutes before serving. *Serves 4*

# Smoked Trout with Cranberry-Pear Salsa

FRAGRANT SMOKED TROUT IS THE PERFECT FOIL FOR THIS HOLIDAY SALSA,
WHICH USES CRANBERRIES FOR A SPECIAL TARTNESS.

1/2 cup frozen cranberries

2 pears, peeled, cored, and diced

Juice of 1 lime

1/2 shallot, minced

1 tablespoon chopped fresh cilantro

2 tablespoons orange juice

1 teaspoon minced orange zest

4 green leaf or red leaf lettuce leaves

12 ounces skinned and boned smoked trout

Coarsely chop the cranberries. In a bowl, combine them with the
pears, lime juice, shallots, cilantro, orange juice, and orange zest.
Stir to mix well.

To serve, arrange the lettuce leaves on 4 plates. Top each
with one-fourth of the smoked trout. Spoon one-fourth of the salsa
alongside. *Serves 4*

# Endive, Stilton, and Raspberry Salad with Raspberry Vinaigrette

SWEET RASPBERRIES BLEND WELL WITH THE CREAMY, SALTY CHEESE AND
THE FAINT BITTERNESS OF IVORY-HUED BELGIAN ENDIVE.

5 heads Belgian endive

1/4 cup raspberry vinegar

1/4 cup extra virgin olive oil

1/2 teaspoon freshly ground black pepper

1/4 teaspoon minced fresh rosemary

2 tablespoons minced fresh parsley

2 cups fresh raspberries

4 ounces Stilton cheese, cut into 4 wedges or slices

Remove the bitter core of the Belgian endive by cutting a cone out of the base of each head. Separate the leaves, setting aside the 2- to 3-inch-long ones. Coarsely chop the larger leaves and set aside.

In a salad bowl, combine the vinegar, olive oil, pepper, and rosemary. With a fork, mix them just until blended. Add the chopped endive, half the whole endive leaves, half the parsley, and half the raspberries. Toss gently to coat. Divide the salad among 4 salad plates. Divide the remaining whole endive leaves, berries, and parsley among the plates, arranging them attractively. Place a wedge or slice of cheese on each plate. *Serves 4*

33

# Jellied Cranberry Salad

A JELLIED SALAD IS A HOLIDAY TRADITION IN MANY AMERICAN HOMES. THIS ONE, COLORED

A BAROQUE CHRISTMAS RED, COMBINES BOTH CRANBERRY SAUCE AND RASPBERRY JELL-O TO GIVE IT AN UNUSUAL FLAVOR

AND A DENSE TEXTURE, WHILE SURPRISING BITS OF SWEETNESS COME FROM THE FRESH PINEAPPLE.

One 16-ounce can
jellied cranberry sauce

2 packages raspberry Jell-O gelatin

1-1/2 cups boiling water

1 teaspoon grated orange zest

1 teaspoon grated lemon zest

1-1/4 cups finely chopped
fresh pineapple, or 10 ounces canned
crushed pineapple, well drained

1/2 cup diced celery

8 lettuce leaves

8 fresh flat-leaf parsley sprigs or
other fresh herb such as sage or mint

In a medium saucepan, heat the cranberry sauce over low heat, stirring occasionally, until it dissolves, about 4 to 5 minutes. In a bowl, combine the Jell-O and boiling water and stir until the gelatin has dissolved. Stir in the melted cranberry sauce, orange and lemon zests, pineapple, and celery.

Pour the mixture into a 9-by-13-inch glass baking dish or into small ramekins or tartlet pans and refrigerate until firm, about 6 hours.

To serve, arrange the lettuce leaves and herb sprigs on 8 plates. Cut the salad into 10 rectangles if using a baking dish. If using ramekins or tartlet pans, unmold gelatin salads by gently loosening gelatin mixture from sides of mold with a small sharp knife. Invert one molded gelatin salad or place one gelatin rectangle onto each lettuce leaf. *Serves 9 to 10*

# tabletop fruit

## 3

# *Fruit Table Wreath*

WHILE THIS SIMPLE WREATH MAY BE HUNG ON THE DOOR, WHEN CANDLES ARE PLACED INSIDE THE WREATH CROWN IT MAKES A GLORIOUS CENTERPIECE FOR A HOLIDAY TABLE.

YOU WILL NEED:

20-gauge green florist's wire

Magnolia or other large green leaves

Wire wreath frame

Hot-glue gun and glue sticks

Lady apples

Magnolia seed pods

Variety of pillar candles

TO MAKE:

Twist wire around each leaf stem, then lay each stem on the wreath frame and twist the wire around the frame to secure it. Overlap the leaves to hide the wired ends, continuing until the frame is covered completely. Hot-glue apples and seed pods directly onto the leaves.

Place the wreath on a small flat tray or cake plate to catch the wax, then place the candles around it and set it in the center of the table.

# *Holiday Fruit Candles*

MAKING THESE CANDLES IS MUCH LIKE CARVING A MINIATURE PUMPKIN, AND AS WITH

A PUMPKIN, THE LIGHT INSIDE GIVES OFF A WELCOME GLOW. PERSONALIZE THE CANDLES BY CARVING

YOUR GUESTS' INITIALS OR CHOOSE A SIMPLE HOLIDAY DESIGN.

YOU WILL NEED:

Paring knife

Large navel oranges

Teaspoon

Orange fine-tip marker pen

X-Acto knife

Small votive candles

Long-handled matches

TO MAKE:

With the paring knife, slice off the top one-quarter of each orange. With the spoon, carefully scoop out the flesh, leaving as much of the inner white pith as possible.

Using the marker, trace a large initial or decorative design on the side of each orange. Using the X-Acto knife, carefully cut out the letter or design.

Until ready to use, seal the finished oranges in a large plastic bag and refrigerate to prevent the hollowed skin from curling.

Place a votive candle inside each orange and place at each table place setting. Light candles with a match just before guests sit down to dine.

# *Fruit Napkin Rings*

FRUIT NAPKIN RINGS THREADED WITH CRANBERRIES AND DECORATED WITH DRIED

SEED PODS MAKE A FESTIVE AND PERSONAL STATEMENT FOR THE TABLE.

YOU WILL NEED:

Fresh cranberries or other non-juicy fruit,
such as kumquats

9-inch lengths of 20-gauge florist's wire

Scissors

Hot-glue gun and glue sticks

Seed or flower pods from the garden,
such as rose hips, sunflower heads, or zinnias

TO MAKE:

Thread the cranberries and other fruit onto the wire, leaving 1 inch of wire free at each end. Place a small dot of hot glue on both sides of each fruit at the point where it is pierced by the wire to seal in any juice that might seep out.

Make a circle of the cranberry wire and twist together the two free ends, snipping off any extra. Hot-glue seed pods in between the fruits in a decorative pattern. Place a napkin through each cranberry ring and place at each setting at your holiday table.

# *Fruit Place Cards*

PLACE CARDS WERE *DE RIGUEUR* DURING THE NINETEENTH AND EARLY TWENTIETH CENTURIES AND ARE STAGING A COMEBACK TODAY. THEY ARE FUN TO MAKE AND ADD A PERSONAL TOUCH TO THE HOLIDAY TABLE.

YOU WILL NEED:

Heavy art or watercolor paper or card stock

Scallop-edged scissors

Fine-point calligraphy pen or marker

Hot-glue gun and glue sticks

Evergreen sprigs, such as fir or pine

Fresh cranberries or other small, hard fruit,
such as kumquats

TO MAKE:

Cut out the desired number of place cards to the size of your choice. Using the calligraphy pen, write the names on the cards. Put a small dot of hot glue on the underside of each sprig and glue the sprigs onto the cards. Put a small dot of hot glue on each fruit and glue the fruit onto each evergreen sprig. Set a card at each place setting.

# *Citrus Tree Centerpieces*

LEMONS AND TANGERINES ARE CLASSIC WINTER FRUITS, WELCOMED BY ALL FOR THEIR

BRIGHT COLORS AND SPRIGHTLY FLAVORS. THESE SIMPLE CENTERPIECES DISPLAY THEM TO THEIR BEST ADVANTAGE.

YOU CAN ALSO USE LIMES FOR AN ALL-GREEN EFFECT.

YOU WILL NEED:

Floral foam blocks

Silver mint julep cups

Sharp knife

Wooden toothpicks

Wooden skewers, about 4 inches long,
for larger fruit

Small lemons

Small tangerines

Evergreen sprigs, such as fir or
pine, with small stem ends intact

TO MAKE:

Soak the floral foam in water. Place a block of foam about 12 inches high in a julep cup, and using the knife, shape the portion of foam above the rim into a cone shape.

Stick the toothpicks into the smaller fruit and the skewers into the larger fruit. Starting at the bottom of the cone, attach the fruit by pushing the picks into the foam, working in circles from the bottom of the cone to the top. Insert evergreen sprigs in between fruit to cover any gaps.

Fruit trees will last up to 2 weeks and can be refrigerated. Do not water or they will mold.

# savory fruit

4

# Whole Smoked Pheasants with Dried Cherry Glaze

THE SLIGHTLY TART TASTE OF DEEP RED CHERRIES AND THE SMOKY FLAVOR FROM A GRILL COMBINE TO IMBUE
THE PHEASANT'S FIRM, WHITE MEAT WITH A HINT OF THE WILD, MAKING THIS AN UNUSUAL HOLIDAY CENTERPIECE.

8 ounces dried cherries

3 cups water

1/4 cup granulated sugar

1 tablespoon lemon juice

1 teaspoon powdered pectin

2 pheasants, 2-1/2 to 3 pounds each

1 teaspoon salt

2 teaspoons freshly ground black pepper

12 fresh thyme sprigs

Put the dried cherries in a saucepan and add the water. Bring to a boil over high heat. Reduce heat to medium-high and continue to cook, stirring occasionally, for about 10 minutes, or until the cherries are rehydrated and the water has reduced by about one-third.

Purée the cherries and strain them, reserving the juice and discarding the cherries. Put the juice in a saucepan and bring to a boil over high heat. Add the sugar, lemon juice, and pectin, and continue to boil, stirring, until a syrup forms and the liquid is reduced by half to make 3/4 cup. Set aside. Prepare a charcoal or wood fire in an outdoor grill with a cover.

Rinse the giblets and tuck them inside the body cavity of the pheasants. Rub the birds inside and out with the salt, pepper, and thyme. Stuff the spent thyme into the body cavities. When the coals are glowing hot, push them to the sides of the grill to make room for a drip pan. Place the drip pan in the center of the grill bed, surrounded by the hot coals. Center the pheasants on the grill over the drip pan. Cover the grill, making sure the vents on the lid and at the bottom are open. An oven thermometer placed on the rack should read approximately 350° to 400°F.

Cook the pheasants for 25 minutes, then add about a dozen more pieces of charcoal. Cook another 20 minutes, or until the skin is golden, and when a sharp knife is inserted into the base of the thigh, the juice runs slightly pink. If you desire a smoky taste, soak some wood chips, such as alder or cherry, in water, and then squeeze them dry. Remove the grill cover, transfer the pheasants to a platter and remove the rack. Scatter the coals with damp wood chips. Replace the grill rack and the pheasant.

Using a pastry brush, paint the pheasants with the cherry glaze mixture and cook another 5 minutes, or until the juices at the base of the thigh run clear.

Transfer the pheasants to a platter and paint them again, making several coats with the glaze. Cover the birds loosely with foil and let stand 10 minutes before serving. Serve whole, accompanied by the remaining dried cherry syrup. Carve at the table. Or carve the breasts into slices, place them on a warm platter along with the leg pieces, and garnish with the syrup. *Serves 6*

# Seared Duck Breast with Orange and Currant Couscous

ORANGE AND DUCK ARE A CLASSIC FLAVOR PAIRING, AND HERE THE TENDER BREASTS ARE PREPARED WITH AN ORANGE MARINADE BEFORE BEING COOKED. THE ORANGES AND CURRANTS IN THE COUSCOUS FURTHER ENHANCE THE COMBINATION.

### MARINADE

1/4 cup fresh orange juice, strained

2 tablespoons red wine vinegar

2 tablespoons extra virgin olive oil

Coarsely chopped zest of 1 orange

1/2 red onion, sliced

1/2 teaspoon salt

1/2 teaspoon freshly ground black pepper

3 or 4 fresh thyme sprigs

2 or 3 fresh rosemary sprigs

6 duck breast halves

### COUSCOUS

1-3/4 cups water

1 teaspoon extra virgin olive oil

1/2 teaspoon salt

2 cups couscous

1/4 cup dried currants

6 orange sections, white pith removed, cut into 4 pieces

2 tablespoons finely grated orange zest

3 tablespoons fresh orange juice, strained

3 tablespoons chopped fresh mint

1 tablespoon extra-virgin olive oil

To make the marinade: In a large bowl or shallow baking dish, mix all the marinade ingredients together. Put the duck breasts in the marinade and turn several times. Cover the dish with plastic wrap and refrigerate, turning occasionally, for 4 to 12 hours.

To make the couscous: In a large saucepan, bring the water to a boil and add the 1 teaspoon olive oil, salt, couscous, and currants, stirring to mix. Remove from heat and let stand for 5 minutes. Using a fork and your fingertips, fluff the couscous to separate it. Taste and adjust for salt. Stir in the oranges, orange zest, orange juice, and mint. Set aside and keep warm or let cool to room temperature.

Remove the breasts from the marinade and pat dry, discarding the marinade. In a large skillet over medium-high heat, heat the remaining olive oil. Add the breasts and cook for 2 to 3 minutes, or until lightly browned. Turn and cook on the other side for 2 to 3 minutes, or until lightly browned. Transfer to a cutting board and cut each breast into 1/4-inch-thick slices. Arrange each sliced breast in a fan shape on a warm dinner plate, accompanied by the couscous. Serve immediately. *Serves 6*

# Grilled Cornish Game Hens with Apple Cider and Brown Sugar Glaze

GRILLED, JUICY GAME HENS, INFUSED WITH THE FLAVOR OF THEIR GLAZE AND THEIR SKIN COLORED
A LOVELY DEEP MAHOGANY, ARE A DIFFERENT TWIST ON THE CLASSIC HOLIDAY BIRD DISH.

GLAZE

1/4 cup apple cider

1/2 cup firmly packed light brown sugar

1 teaspoon Dijon-style mustard

1 tablespoon cider vinegar

2 Rock Cornish game hens

1/2 teaspoon salt

1 teaspoon freshly ground black pepper

1 clove garlic, minced

8 fresh thyme sprigs

4 winter savory sprigs

To make the glaze: In a small saucepan, combine the cider and sugar and bring to a boil over medium-high heat, stirring to dissolve the sugar. When the sugar is dissolved, add the mustard and continue to cook, stirring, until it is thickened and reduced by about one-third. Remove from heat and stir in the cider vinegar. Set aside.

Prepare a charcoal or wood fire in an outdoor grill. Remove the giblets from the game hens and discard or reserve for another use. Rub the hens inside and out with the salt, pepper, and garlic, and stuff each bird with sprigs of the fresh herbs. Place them breast-side down over a medium-hot fire—the coals should be glowing—and sear for 2 to 3 minutes. Turn and sear on the other side for 2 to 3 minutes. Continue to grill, turning often, for another 8 to 10 minutes. Using tongs, transfer the birds to a platter.

Remove the grill rack from the grill and set aside. Push the coals to the sides of the grill to make room for a drip pan. Center the drip pan in the bottom of the grill, surrounded by the hot coals. Replace the grill rack.

Using a pastry brush, baste the hot birds on both sides with the glaze, then return them to the grill, placing them breast-side up, over the drip pan. Baste again with the glaze. Put the cover on the grill, making sure the vents on the lid and at the bottom are open. Cook another 2 to 3 minutes, then brush with the glaze again. Repeat 3 more times, for a total cooking time of 12 to 15 minutes, or until the flesh is white and firm and the skin is a crisp and glistening mahogany color. Transfer to a platter, remove the herb sprigs, and cover loosely with foil and let rest for 10 minutes. Serve whole, or cut in half with a knife or poultry shears. *Serves 4*

# Roast Turkey with Dried Fig and Apricot Stuffing

FRUITS, DRIED IN SUMMER AT THEIR PEAK OF SWEETNESS, APPEAR ON HOLIDAY TABLES IN MANY FORMS YEAR-ROUND.

HERE, THEY ARE AN INTEGRAL PART OF THE *PIÈCE DE RÉSISTANCE*, STUFFED TURKEY.

## STUFFING

5 to 6 cups of day-old baguette,
pain au levain, Italian slipper bread, or any combination
of country-style breads, torn into large pieces

1-1/2 tablespoons unsalted butter

1 onion, finely chopped (about 1 cup)

1 garlic clove, minced

2-1/2 cups boiling chicken broth

1/2 cup chopped dried figs

3/4 cup chopped dried apricots

3 tablespoons minced fresh rosemary

3 tablespoons minced fresh thyme

1 teaspoon salt

1 teaspoons freshly ground black pepper

One 12- to 14-pound turkey

1 teaspoon salt

1-1/2 teaspoons freshly ground black pepper

2 to 3 fresh sage sprigs

## GRAVY

Reserved neck and giblets from turkey

1 carrot, coarsely chopped

1 celery stalk, coarsely chopped

1 large onion, coarsely chopped

2 fresh bay leaves or 1 dried

1/2 teaspoon salt

1/2 teaspoon freshly ground black pepper

4 cups chicken broth

1/4 cup sherry or port

1 portobello mushroom, cut into small cubes

1/4 cup water

3 tablespoons cornstarch

—continued on page 56—

54

To make the stuffing: Put the bread in a large bowl and set aside. In a small saucepan, melt the butter over medium heat. Add the onion and garlic and sauté until translucent, 3 to 4 minutes. Add the boiling broth and pour the mixture over the bread. Turn the bread to make sure that all the pieces become soaked. Let stand for 10 to 15 minutes, or until the bread is cool enough to handle and the broth has been absorbed. Squeeze the bread in your hands, further breaking it down, until a thick paste forms. Add the dried fruit, herbs, salt, and pepper and continue squeezing to incorporate them into the paste.

Preheat an oven to 325°F. Remove the neck and giblets from the turkey and set aside. Rub the turkey inside and out with the salt, pepper, and sage. Fill the body and neck cavities loosely with the stuffing. Do not pack tightly, as the stuffing will expand during cooking. Fasten the flaps with turkey skewers, or sew closed using a trussing needle and kitchen thread. Tie the legs together at the bottom, using kitchen thread.

Place the turkey, breast side up, in a rack in a roasting pan and roast for 12 to 15 minutes per pound, basting it often with the pan drippings. When the breast is golden, cover the turkey loosely with aluminum foil. Continue to cook, basting the legs, until a thermometer registers 175° to 180°F in the thickest part of the thigh (near the body but not touching the bone). Remove and let stand for about 20 minutes, loosely covered with the foil, before carving.

To make the gravy: In a medium saucepan, combine the neck, all the giblets except the liver, carrot, celery, onion, bay leaves, salt, pepper, and broth. Bring to a boil, then reduce heat to low and simmer, uncovered, for about 1 hour, or until the neck meat is cooked and can be removed easily with a fork. Add the liver and cook another 4 to 5 minutes, or just until the liver is cooked through.

Pour the contents of the pan though a sieve, reserving the broth, neck, and giblets and discarding the vegetables. Remove the giblets and mince them. Remove the neck meat and mince it as well. Set aside. Add enough water to the reserved broth to make 4 cups. Return it to the saucepan and add the sherry and the mushroom. Simmer over medium-high heat for 3 to 4 minutes, or until the mushrooms are cooked through. Set aside until ready to serve.

When the turkey is done, pour off the fat from the roasting pan. Heat the pan on top of the stove. Pour in the reserved broth, giblet and neck meat, and mushroom mixture, stirring to scrape up any browned bits. In a small bowl, combine the water and cornstarch and mix well. Add this mixture to the pan, stirring until a smooth, thick gravy forms, about 1 minute. Taste and adjust the seasoning. Serve alongside the turkey. *Serves 10 to 12*

# Whipped Sweet Potatoes with Caramelized Tangerine Topping

SWEET POTATOES ARE A HOLIDAY STAPLE ON MANY TABLES, AND WHEN GIVEN A SWEET TOPPING OF HONEY-CARAMELIZED TANGERINES, THE TEMPTATION IS TO EAT MORE THAN YOUR SHARE.

2-1/2 pounds sweet potatoes

3 tablespoons butter

1/2 teaspoon ground cinnamon

1/4 cup heavy cream

TOPPING

3 tablespoons honey

1 tablespoon unsalted butter

3 tangerines, peeled, seeded, sectioned, and coarsely chopped

1/2 cup chopped walnuts

Preheat an oven to 350°F. Pierce the sweet potatoes several times with a fork and put them on a baking sheet and bake for 1 hour, or until very soft when pierced with a small knife. Remove from the oven and let cool to the touch. Peel off the skin and discard.

In a large bowl, combine the sweet potatoes, butter, cinnamon, and cream, and using an electric mixer, whip on medium speed. Butter an oven-to-table baking dish and put the whipped potatoes in it.

To make the topping: In a small skillet, combine the honey and butter and heat over medium-low heat until the butter melts. Add the chopped tangerines and walnuts and cook, stirring, for 3 to 4 minutes, or until the fruit is softened, somewhat translucent, and lightly caramelized. Spoon this topping over the whipped potatoes and bake for 20 minutes, or until the top is slightly golden and the potatoes are thoroughly hot. Serve immediately. *Serves 4 to 6*

# Salmon Fillets with Persimmon-Lime Salsa

FUYU PERSIMMONS AND PALE HONEYDEW MELON MAKE A COLORFUL COMPLEMENT TO SALMON IN THIS SWEET AND TANGY SALSA FLAVORED WITH LIME, SHALLOTS, AND CILANTRO. GARNISH WITH LIME WEDGES WHEN SERVING.

### SALSA

2 Fuyu persimmons, seeded and diced

2 cups diced honeydew melon

1/4 teaspoon salt

1/4 teaspoon freshly ground black pepper

1/4 cup fresh lime juice

2 tablespoons finely grated lime zest

2 tablespoons minced shallots

1/4 cup minced fresh cilantro

1/2 teaspoon salt

1/4 teaspoon freshly ground black pepper

1/8 teaspoon cayenne pepper

4 salmon fillets, each about 4 to 5 ounces

1 tablespoon unsalted butter

1 lime, halved,
plus additional wedges for serving

To make the salsa: In a medium bowl, combine all the salsa ingredients and mix well. Cover and refrigerate for 2 to 6 hours. In a bowl, combine the salt, black pepper, and cayenne pepper and mix well. Rub each salmon fillet with the mixture. In a large skillet, melt the butter over medium-high heat until it foams. Add the salmon and cook for 2 minutes. Reduce heat to medium, turn, and cook on the other side for another 2 to 3 minutes, or until the fish flakes easily with a fork. Squeeze the juice of the lime over it. Serve immediately, topped with a spoonful of the salsa. Serve the remaining salsa alongside. *Serves 4*

# Savory Apple-Herb Galettes

THESE LIGHT, FLAVORFUL PANCAKE-LIKE GALETTES TASTE LIKE FRESH APPLES AND ARE THE PERFECT ACCOMPANIMENT

TO MEATS SUCH AS GRILLED CORNISH GAME HENS (PAGE 53), PORK CHOPS, OR CHICKEN. YOU CAN ADJUST THE FLAVOR BY

CHOOSING SWEET APPLES, SUCH AS GOLDEN DELICIOUS OR GALA, OR TART ONES, SUCH AS GRANNY SMITH.

2 apples, cored, peeled, and coarsely grated

1 egg, lightly beaten

1/4 cup all-purpose flour

1/8 teaspoon salt

1/4 teaspoon freshly ground black pepper

1/4 teaspoon minced fresh thyme

1/4 teaspoon minced fresh sage

2 tablespoons unsalted butter

In a bowl, combine all the ingredients except the butter and stir to mix. In a large skillet, melt the butter over medium heat. When the butter foams, drop in a bit of the batter. If it sizzles, the skillet is hot enough. If not, wait a few seconds and try again. When the skillet is hot, drop heaping tablespoons of the batter in it, allowing 1 inch between each galette. Cook for 1 to 2 minutes, or until golden on the bottom and set. Turn and cook 1 minute more, or just until golden. Transfer to a plate and keep warm. Repeat to use all the remaining batter. *Makes 12 to 14 cakes; Serves 4 to 6*

# decorative fruit

5

# Holiday Fruit Wreath

A BEAUTIFUL WREATH TO HANG OUTSIDE OR IN IS A PREREQUISITE FOR THE HOLIDAY SEASON. HERE, WE HAVE CHOSEN TO MAKE THE BASE OF THE WREATH WITH ROSE HIPS AND TO DECORATE IT WITH SMALL WINTER CITRUS AND COLORED LEAVES.

## YOU WILL NEED:

20-gauge florist's wire

Branches of large rose hips

12-inch wire wreath frame

Hot-glue gun and glue sticks

Small satsuma mandarins or kumquats

Small fall leaves

24-inch length of 1-inch wide ribbon for hanging the wreath

## TO MAKE:

Wire single rose-hip stems into clusters. Wire the rose-hip clusters onto the wreath frame, overlapping each new cluster over the stem ends of the previous cluster to cover all the stem ends.

Hot-glue the mandarins or kumquats onto the rose hips and space them evenly around the frame. Hot-glue the leaves in a scattered pattern around the wreath and tuck a few under the fruit and between the rose hips.

Loop the ribbon around the top of the wreath and hang on a door, window, wall, or mirror.

# Dried-Fruit Christmas Tree Ornaments

IT'S FUN TO CREATE NEW ORNAMENTS EACH YEAR FOR CHRISTMAS, AND THESE ARE ATTRACTIVE,

SEASONAL, AND EASY FOR CHILDREN TO STRING.

YOU WILL NEED:

Baking sheets

Parchment paper

Sharp knife

Oranges, lemons, apples

Waxed paper

Copper wire

Wire cutters

Cinnamon sticks

Decorative ribbons

Scissors

Fuyu persimmon tops, and crab apples with stems

TO MAKE:

Preheat an oven to 200°F. Line baking sheets with parchment paper.

Using the knife, slice the citrus and apples very thinly, about 1/4 inch thick, and lay on the prepared sheets in a single layer. To make whole dried oranges or lemons, cut vertical slits 1/2 to 3/4 inches apart around the fruit. Bake for 1-1/2 to 2 hours, or until the white pith has dried and the fruits are leathery but not crisp. Remove and let cool to room temperature. Store in an airtight tin in single layers, separated by waxed paper.

Using the copper wire, thread the fruit slices singly or together in pairs into numerous ornaments. Slices can be topped with cinnamon sticks or decorative ribbons. Thread fresh crab apple stems with persimmon tops and twist pieces of copper wire around stems for hanging.

Cut additional 6-inch lengths of copper wire and use them to attach the other ornaments to the tree.

# Dried-Fruit Christmas Tree

A FRESH EVERGREEN TREE HUNG WITH DRIED-FRUIT
ORNAMENTS IS THE PERFECT HOLIDAY DECORATION FOR
THOSE WHO APPRECIATE NATURE'S SPLENDORS.

YOU WILL NEED:

Handsaw

Evergreen Christmas tree

Floral foam blocks

Sharp knife

Plastic bucket that fits inside decorative container

Large decorative container to hold tree and foam

Dried-fruit ornaments (see page 67)

TO MAKE:

Using the saw, cut the tree to the desired height. Using the knife,
cut the foam blocks to fill the bucket.

Place the foam-filled bucket in the decorative container and
fill with water to soak the foam. Drain off the water and insert the
tree trunk into the center of the foam. Adjust and straighten the
tree as necessary. Hang the fruit ornaments on the branches.

# *Fruit, Herb, and Spice Potpourri*

POTPOURRI IS NOT DIFFICULT TO MAKE AND CAN BE PERSONALIZED TO REFLECT YOUR

TASTE AND SENSIBILITIES BY ADDING MORE OF ONE INGREDIENT THAN ANOTHER.

YOU WILL NEED:

Dried-fruit peels, herbs, and spices
(available from a grocery or floral supply store), such as:

Orange and lemon peels

Star anise pods

Cinnamon chips

Bay leaves

Whole nutmeg

Hibiscus flowers

Rose hips

Freeze-dried orange slices

Cedar needles

Lavender florets

Shallow decorative bowl or box

TO MAKE:

Combine the ingredients and place in a bowl or box and set in a room.

# Fruit and Pinecone Garlands

GARLANDS ARE AMONG THE MOST FESTIVE OF DECORATIONS AND CAN BE HUNG ABOVE MIRRORS, PAINTINGS, MANTLES, OR DOORS TO WELCOME THE HOLIDAY SEASON.

YOU WILL NEED:

Electric drill and 1/16-inch drill bit

Small pinecones

Wire cutters

20-gauge florist's wire

Fresh cranberries

TO MAKE:

Using the electric drill, make a small hole at the base of each pinecone. Using the wire cutters, cut a piece of wire to the length that you wish your garland to be.

Twist a small loop in one end of the wire, then begin threading the pine cones and berries onto the wire from the other end. Alternate a pinecone, then 3 to 5 berries, repeating until the wire is full. Leave 2 inches of bare wire at the end of the garland and twist into another loop.

Hang the garland from the loop ends or around a mirror, a painting, a mantle or a doorway.

# fruit desserts

6

# Baked Apples with Maple-Bourbon Filling

FIRM, TART APPLES ARE BEST FOR BAKING BECAUSE THEY HOLD THEIR SHAPE WELL. FOR A SPECIAL OCCASION, SERVE THESE WITH MAPLE-NUT ICE CREAM OR WHIPPED CREAM THAT HAS BEEN LIGHTLY FLAVORED WITH BOURBON AND VANILLA.

4 large, firm, tart apples, such as Granny Smith or McIntosh

1/2 cup firmly packed light brown sugar

1/4 cup chopped hazelnuts or walnuts

2 tablespoons maple syrup

2 tablespoons bourbon

2 teaspoons butter, cut into 4 pieces

Preheat an oven to 350°F. Core the apples, but stop about 1/2 inch from the bottom. Set aside. In a bowl, combine the brown sugar, nuts, syrup, and bourbon and mix well. Spoon the mixture into each apple core. Dot with the butter.

Put the filled apples in a deep baking dish just large enough to hold them. Pour water into the dish to cover the bottom about 1/4 inch deep. Cover with a lid or seal tightly with aluminum foil and bake for 30 minutes, basting twice with the pan juices. Remove the cover, baste again with the juices and cook, basting once or twice more, another 10 minutes, or until the thickest part of the apple is tender and can easily be pierced with the tip of a sharp knife.

Transfer the apples to individual dessert plates or a serving platter and spoon the now-thickened pan juices over them. Serve hot, warm, or at room temperature. *Serves 4*

# Mango Cheesecake with Graham Cracker Crust

MANGOS HAVE A DELICIOUSLY SWEET FLAVOR AND A SOFT TEXTURE THAT BLENDS WELL WITH CREAM CHEESE

FOR A TROPICAL CHEESECAKE GARNISHED WITH MACADAMIA NUTS.

### CRUST

3-1/4 cups finely ground graham crackers
(about 10 to 12 ounces crackers or about
54 2-inch-by-2-inch crackers)

1/4 cup granulated sugar

4 to 5 tablespoons butter, melted

### FILLING

Two 8-ounce packages cream cheese
at room temperature

3/4 cup firmly packed brown sugar

2 eggs

2-1/2 to 3 pounds ripe mangos,
peeled, cut from the pit, and puréed
(about 3-1/2 cups)

1/2 cup heavy cream

2 teaspoons fresh lime juice

1/2 to 3/4 cup crushed macadamia nuts

To make the crust: Preheat an oven to 325°F. In a small bowl, combine all the ingredients. Press the mixture over the bottom of a 9-by-2-1/2-inch round springform pan. Using your fingertips, push all but a thin coating toward the sides of the pan. Pressing with your fingertips, make a crust about 1-1/2 inches up the sides of the pan; the edges will be slightly irregular. Bake until lightly browned, about 15 minutes. Let cool on a wire rack, then chill thoroughly in the refrigerator before filling.

To make the filling: In a large bowl, combine the cream cheese and brown sugar. Using an electric mixer, beat them together until well blended. Beat in the eggs, one at a time, until the mixture is smooth and well blended.

In a medium bowl, combine the mango purée, cream, and lime juice, and using a spoon, mix until well blended. Add the mango mixture to the cream cheese mixture and mix until well blended. Pour the filling into the crust and bake for about 50 minutes, or until the center barely moves when jiggled.

Let cool on a wire rack, then refrigerate at least overnight before serving. To serve, run a knife around the edge of the pan, then release the sides, leaving the bottom of the pan in place. Serve chilled, sprinkled with the crushed nuts. *Makes one 9-inch cake; serves 12*

# Pear and Quince Crisp

SWEET PEARS AND QUINCES, WITH THEIR FAINTLY CITRUS TASTE, COMBINE TO MAKE A JUICY CRISP,
COVERED WITH A FRAGRANT TOPPING SCENTED WITH SPICES.

### TOPPING

1-1/4 cups all-purpose flour

1/4 teaspoon salt

1/4 teaspoon ground mace

1/8 teaspoon ground cardamom

1 teaspoon grated lemon zest

1/2 cup firmly packed light brown sugar

2 tablespoons granulated sugar

3 tablespoons butter, cut into small bits

1-1/2 pounds pears, peeled and cored

1-1/2 pounds quinces, peeled and cored

2 tablespoons fresh lemon juice

1/2 cup granulated sugar

2 tablespoons all-purpose flour

Preheat an oven to 375°F To make the topping: In a medium bowl, combine all the ingredients and mix together with your fingertips just enough to form a crumbly mixture. Set aside.

Grease an 8-inch square baking dish. Cut the pears and the quinces lengthwise into 1/2-inch-thick slices. Put them in a bowl and stir in the lemon juice, sugar, and flour. Put the fruit mixture in the prepared dish.

Sprinkle the topping over the top of the fruit mixture. Bake for 30 to 35 minutes, or until the top is golden brown and the fruit and its juices are bubbling. *Serves 8*

# Pears Poached in Red Wine with Raspberry Sauce

PEARS ARE ONE OF THE FAVORITE FRUITS OF AUTUMN AND WINTER, AND WHEN POACHED IN RED WINE AND DRESSED WITH

A SWEETLY TART SAUCE OF RED RASPBERRIES, THEY MAKE A FESTIVE AND COLORFUL CONCLUSION TO A MEAL.

4 cups dry red wine, such as merlot,
pinot noir, or zinfandel

2 cups granulated sugar

One 3-inch piece vanilla bean, halved lengthwise

4 ripe but firm pears, peeled, halved, and cored

RASPBERRY SAUCE

3 cups fresh or frozen raspberries

1/2 cup granulated sugar

1/4 cup water

In a large saucepan, combine the wine, sugar, and vanilla bean. Bring to a boil over medium-high heat, stirring constantly until the sugar is dissolved. Boil for 3 to 4 minutes more, or until the liquid is slightly thickened. Reduce heat to low and add the pear halves. Poach them for 7 to 8 minutes, or until they are tender but still hold their shape. Remove from heat. Discard the vanilla bean.

With a slotted spoon, transfer the pears to a bowl and pour the poaching liquid over them. Let cool to room temperature, about 20 minutes, turning them from time to time. (The longer the pears stand in the poaching liquid, the more they will absorb and the darker they will become. They can stand for several hours, or if refrigerated, up to 24 hours before serving. If you want to serve the pears warm after they have been refrigerated, pour the poaching liquid back into a saucepan and heat over medium heat. Reduce heat to low, add the pears, and simmer 2 to 3 minutes, or just long enough to warm the pears.)

To make the sauce: If using fresh raspberries, reserve a few for garnish. In a medium saucepan, combine all the ingredients, and mashing the berries with the back of a wooden spoon, cook over high heat for about 5 minutes. Reduce heat to low and continue to cook, stirring often, another 5 minutes. Put a bowl beneath a food mill, then put the berries through the mill to remove the seeds, scraping the bottom of the mill to make sure you get all the pulp as well as the juice. Return the juice and pulp to the saucepan. Cook over medium heat just until the sauce thickens a bit and warms, 2 to 3 minutes.

Arrange 2 warm or chilled pear halves on each dessert plate and pour a tablespoon or so of the poaching liquid over them, then a spoonful of the raspberry sauce. Garnish with a few whole raspberries, if available. *Serves 4*

# Glazed Orange Tart

THIS REFRESHING AND UNUSUAL TART IS AN IDEAL USE OF THIS POPULAR WINTERTIME FRUIT.

THE DELICATE ORANGE FLAVOR OF THE CUSTARD IS ENHANCED BY THE GLAZED ORANGE ROUNDS ON TOP.

LEMON MAY BE USED INSTEAD OF ORANGES, AND INDIVIDUAL TARTS MAY BE MADE AS WELL.

## CRUST

2 cups all-purpose flour

1/2 teaspoon salt

1/2 cup (1 stick) plus 1 tablespoon cold unsalted butter

6 tablespoons ice water

## FILLING

2-1/4 cups granulated sugar

1 cup water

2 oranges, cut into 1/4-inch-thick rounds, seeds removed

1/3 cup cornstarch

1/4 teaspoon salt

1-1/2 cups boiling water

3 egg yolks, in a bowl

1/3 cup fresh orange juice, strained

2 tablespoons butter

2 teaspoons grated orange zest

To make the crust: Preheat an oven to 425°F. In a bowl, combine the flour and salt. Cut the butter into 1/2-inch chunks and add them to the flour mixture. With a pastry blender or 2 knives, cut the flour into the butter until pea-sized balls form. Add the ice water 1 tablespoon at a time, turning the dough lightly with a fork and then with your fingertips. This will help to keep the pastry light and flaky. Do not overwork the dough, or it will become tough. Gather the dough into a ball—it will be a little crumbly—wrap it in plastic wrap, and refrigerate for 15 minutes.

On a floured surface, roll out the dough 1/8-inch thick and about 14 inches in diameter. Roll up the pastry around the rolling pin, then gently unroll it over a 12-inch tart pan. Push the pastry into the pan to fit and trim off any excess dough. Line the pan with aluminum foil and partially fill with pie weights or dried beans.

Bake for 12 to 15 minutes, or until set but not colored. Remove from the oven and take off the foil and weights. Prick any bubbles with the tines of a fork and return to the oven for 5 minutes, or until barely colored. Remove and set aside.

To make the filling: In a saucepan, combine 1 cup of the sugar and the water and bring to a boil over high heat, stirring to dissolve the sugar. Reduce heat to medium and add the oranges.

—continued on next page—

# Glazed Orange Tart

Cook, turning occasionally, for about 20 minutes, or until the oranges and their rinds have turned a darker color. Remove from heat and set aside, leaving the oranges in the syrup.

In the top of a double boiler, combine the cornstarch, the remaining 1-1/4 cups sugar, and the salt over boiling water. Add the 1-1/2 cups boiling water and mix well with a whisk. Remove the pan from the double boiler and cook the mixture over direct heat, stirring constantly until it becomes thick and changes to a clearer color, about 10 minutes.

Add a little of the hot cornstarch mixture to the egg yolks and stir to mix well, then pour the egg yolks into the cornstarch mixture and return it to the double boiler. Cook for 2 minutes more, stirring continuously. Remove from heat and stir in the orange juice, butter, and orange zest, mixing well. Let cool for 5 to 10 minutes, then spoon the mixture into the tart pan and top with the sliced orange rounds. Spoon 1 tablespoon of the syrup over the oranges.

Reduce the heat to 350°F and bake the pie another 10 minutes to form a glaze on the surface. Remove from the oven. Serve warm. *Makes one 12-inch tart; serves 10*

# Cranberry Sorbet

WITH EACH ICY BITE, CHUNKY BITS OF CRANBERRIES DELIVER A BURST OF TART FLAVOR. SERVE WITH FAVORITE HOLIDAY COOKIES OR BISCOTTI.

2 cups fresh or frozen cranberries

1/4 cup fresh orange juice

3 cups water

1 cup granulated sugar

1 tablespoon fresh lemon juice

1 tablespoon grated orange zest

In a saucepan, combine the cranberries, orange juice, and 1/2 cup of the water. Cook over medium heat until cranberries pop open, 5 to 7 minutes. Coarsely mash the cranberries, still in the saucepan, with the back of wooden spoon. (You should have about 1-1/2 cups purée.) Add the sugar, lemon juice, orange zest, and remaining water. Bring to a boil over medium-high heat. Reduce heat to low and simmer, stirring often, until a syrup forms, about 15 minutes.

Let cool and refrigerate for at least 6 hours, or as long as overnight. Freeze in an ice cream maker according to the manufacturer's instructions. *Makes about 1 quart*

# Frozen Sherbet-Filled Oranges, Limes, or Lemons

THESE MEDITERRANEAN-STYLE FROZEN CITRUS TREATS MAKE A VERY IMPRESSIVE DESSERT,
APPRECIATED BY BOTH ADULTS AND CHILDREN ALIKE. SERVE THE COLORFUL FILLED FRUIT SHELLS IN INDIVIDUAL
COMPOTE DISHES OR TOGETHER ON A PRETTY HOLIDAY PLATTER OR TRAY.

16 sweet oranges, 25 lemons, or 25 limes

2 cups water

2-3/4 cups granulated sugar

1 tablespoon grated orange, lemon,
or lime zest

2 egg whites

Cut off the upper one-fourth to one-third of 6 of the fruits and just enough of the bottom to allow each fruit to sit upright. Don't cut into the pulp. Reserve the tops. Using a spoon, scoop out the pulp, leaving the rinds intact to form shells. Set the pulp, hollowed-out shells, and the tops in the refrigerator to chill.

Juice the remaining fruits, then strain the juice; you should have about 4 cups.

In a large saucepan, combine the juice, water, sugar, and zest and bring to a boil over medium-high heat. Boil, stirring often, until the sugar is dissolved, about 5 minutes. Remove from heat and set aside to cool. While the mixture is cooling, put the egg whites into a medium bowl, and using a hand mixer or whisk, beat until stiff, glossy peaks form. Set aside. When the fruit mixture is cool, pour it into a large bowl and gently fold in the egg whites until well blended.

Transfer the mixture to an ice cream maker and freeze according to the manufacturer's directions. When the mixture has begun to harden, stir in the chilled fruit pulp and continue to freeze until firm but not fully hardened. Spoon the sherbet into the fruit shells, dividing it evenly among them. Place the shells on a plate or pan lined with waxed paper or aluminum foil, add the reserved tops, and freeze for 2 to 3 hours before serving. *Serves 6*

# fruit gifts

7

# Mini Fruit Baskets

FRUIT BASKETS FILLED TO THE BRIM WITH SMALL, SEASONAL
FRUITS, SUCH AS KUMQUATS, LIMES, MANDARINS, SECKEL PEARS, OR
LADY APPLES, MAKE FRAGRANT AND ATTRACTIVE GIFTS.

YOU WILL NEED:

Wooden fruit baskets, 2 per gift (available at crafts stores)

Quantities of small or miniature fruits, such as
lady apples, Seckel pears, kumquats, limes, or mandarins

Adhesive tape

Roll of 1/4-inch-wide ribbon or twine

Gift tags

Hot-glue gun and glue sticks

Sprigs of evergreen or fall leaves

TO MAKE:

Pack a basket with the fruit, piling as much as possible on top.
Place another basket, inverted, on top to form a lid, and add
more fruit under the rim until it is as full as possible.

Tape the baskets on opposite sides of the rim to hold them
together while they are being tied. Tie a ribbon or length of twine
tightly around the two baskets to hold them securely. Remove
the tape.

Tie the top of the ribbon or twine into a bow and thread a
gift tag onto the bow. Hot-glue a sprig of evergreen or a fall leaf
to the ribbon alongside an additional piece of fruit.

# Decorative Preserves

EVERYONE APPRECIATES PRESERVES, JELLIES, AND JAMS FOR THE HOLIDAYS, ESPECIALLY WHEN THOUGHTFULLY DECORATED.

YOU WILL NEED:

Jelly jars

Preserves, marmalades, jellies, or jams

Decorative paper

Rubber cement

Decorative ribbon, color-coordinated
with the preserves

Hot-glue gun and glue sticks

Fresh, dried, or candied fruit similar to
ingredients in preserves

Canning labels

Antique milk bottle carrier (available at
antique stores and flea markets)

Decorative gift tags

TO MAKE:

If making from scratch, fill the jelly jars with preserves. Cut rounds of decorative paper, and using the rubber cement, glue them lightly to the top of the jar lids.

Tie ribbon in small clusters or bows. Hot-glue the fruit decorations to the top of the ribbon clusters or bows. Hot-glue fruit and ribbon decorations to the top of the paper on the jar lids.

Attach canning labels to the jars and tie more ribbon around the neck of each jar. Place the jars in an antique carrier and attach the gift tags.

ginger preserves

# Dried-Fruit Gift Tins

IF POSSIBLE, FIND MILLINERY FRUIT THAT MATCHES THE FRUIT IN THE TINS

SO THAT THE RECIPIENT HAS A CLUE TO THE CONTENTS.

YOU WILL NEED:

Metal tins in different sizes and shapes

Dried fruit, such as apples, apricots, raisins,
dates, or cherries

Scissors

Roll of 1/4-inch-wide ribbon

Adhesive tape

Millinery fruit and leaves (available at crafts stores)

Gift tags

TO MAKE:

Pack the metal tins with your favorite dried fruit and cover tightly
with the lids.

With the scissors, cut a length of ribbon that will tie around
the tin into a bow. Tape the ribbon at its midpoint securely to the
bottom of the tin. Bring the ribbon around the tin and tie into a
knot on top.

Wrap a cluster of millinery fruit and leaves around the knot
and tie the ribbon into a bow, securing the millinery fruit. Thread a
gift tag onto the ribbon ends, if desired.

# Fruit Recipe and Baking Dish

FRESH FRUIT PLACED IN AN ATTRACTIVE BAKING OR PIE DISH,

ALONG WITH THE RECIPE, MAKE A UNIQUE GIFT TO GIVE TO A HOLIDAY HOSTESS,

OR TO BE LEFT ON A NEIGHBOR'S DOORSTEP FOR A HOLIDAY SURPRISE.

YOU WILL NEED:

Fresh fruit

Decorative baking dish, such as
a ceramic baking or pie dish

Your favorite baked-fruit dessert recipe

Pen

Decorative card stock

Hole punch

Scissors

Decorative ribbon

Gift tag

TO MAKE:

Place the fresh fruit in the dish. Write your favorite dessert recipe
on a piece of decorative card stock and punch a hole in one corner.
   Thread the ribbon through the recipe card and tie it into a
bow around the dish handle or the rim of the dish. Attach a gift
tag, if desired.

cinnamon
pear
vinegar

# Fruit Vinegar Gifts

HOMEMADE FRUIT VINEGARS ARE A WELCOME GIFT FOR THE HOLIDAYS. TWO RECIPES ARE GIVEN HERE, BUT YOU MIGHT

SUBSTITUTE OTHER FRUITS, SUCH AS RASPBERRIES, BLACKBERRIES, OR EVEN FIGS.

YOU WILL NEED:

Cinnamon-Pear Vinegar:
2 cups apple cider vinegar, 2 cinnamon sticks,
and 1/2 teaspoon pear-flavored syrup

Pomegranate Vinegar:
2 cups red wine vinegar and 1 cup pomegranate seeds
or 1 tablespoon pomegranate syrup

Funnel

Tall decorative bottles

Pen

Decorative labels

Hole punch

Decorative cord or ribbon

Antique milk bottle carrier
(available at antique stores and flea markets)

Seasonal fresh fruit
(pears and pomegranates are used here)

TO MAKE:

For the Cinnamon-Pear Vinegar: In a nonreactive saucepan, combine the vinegar,  cinnamon sticks, and the pear syrup and bring to a boil over medium heat. Remove from heat and let stand for at least 1 or up to 3 hours.

For the Pomegranate Vinegar: In a nonreactive saucepan, combine the vinegar and pomegranate seeds or syrup and bring to a boil over medium heat. Remove from heat and let stand for at least 1 or up to 3 hours.

Using the funnel, fill the bottles with vinegar and seal them. For decoration, you can add a few cinnamon sticks or pear slices to the Cinnamon-Pear Vinegar or uncooked pomegranate seeds to the Pomegranate Vinegar.

Write the name of each vinegar on a decorative label, hole-punch the label, and thread it with cord or ribbon. Tie labels to the bottle necks and put the bottles in the bottle carrier. Fill the remaining compartments of the carrier with fresh fruit.

fruit drinks

8

# Winter Fruit Apéritifs

APÉRITIFS, WHICH ARE SO POPULAR IN THE MEDITERRANEAN REGION, ESPECIALLY IN FRANCE AND ITALY, ARE SERVED BEFORE A MEAL TO PIQUE THE APPETITE. THEY MAY BE EITHER ALCOHOL-BASED OR SIMPLE FRUIT DRINKS. UNLIKE COCKTAILS, THEY ARE RARELY BASED ON STRONG SPIRITS, WHICH TEND TO DULL THE APPETITE RATHER THAN WHET IT.

2 grapefruits

4 blood oranges

4 navel oranges

4 fresh mint sprigs for garnish

Squeeze the citrus fruits and strain the juice through a fine-meshed sieve into a pitcher. Discard the seeds and pulp. Pour into glasses and serve immediately, garnished with mint. *Makes about 1 quart; serves 4*

# Hot Mulled Wine with Oranges and Lemons

HOT MULLED WINE CONJURES IMAGES OF COLD NIGHTS AND CHRISTMAS CAROLS. IT IS A SPECIAL HOLIDAY TREAT THAT IS FRAGRANT AND EASY TO MAKE.

1 bottle (750 ml) merlot or other light red wine

1/4 cup granulated sugar

2 cinnamon sticks

6 whole cloves

2 star anise pods

1 orange, sliced, seeds removed, plus 8 orange twists

1 lemon, sliced, seeds removed

In a nonreactive saucepan, combine all the ingredients except the orange twists. Cook over medium-high heat until steaming, stirring until the sugar is dissolved. Reduce heat to low and simmer, uncovered, for 30 minutes. To serve, ladle into cups and garnish with an orange twist. *Makes about eight 4-ounce servings*

# Lemon-Scented White Wine

1 lemon

1 whole clove

1 bottle dry white wine, such as
sauvignon blanc or chardonnay

1 cup granulated sugar

1/4 cup brandy

Using a vegetable peeler or zester, remove the zest from the lemon in wide strips. Place the clove in a strip of zest and set aside. Using a knife, remove and discard all but a thin layer of the white pith from the lemon. Cut the lemon crosswise into 6 slices, each about 1/4 inch thick, and set aside.

In a large, nonreactive saucepan, combine the wine, sugar, clove, and all the lemon zest strips. Bring to a simmer over medium heat, stirring to dissolve the sugar, 4 to 5 minutes. Remove from the heat and discard the clove and lemon zest.

In a small saucepan, warm the brandy over low heat. Add the brandy to the wine, pouring it carefully across the surface, then ignite it with a long match. Let it burn until the flames die.

Let cool to room temperature. Serve at room temperature, or cover and refrigerate for at least 2 hours to chill. Serve, in wineglasses garnished with a lemon slice, within 24 hours. *Serves 6 to 8*

# Spiced Apple Cider

APPLE CIDER, SIMMERING ON THE STOVE WITH
SPICES AND FILLING THE KITCHEN WITH AN ENTICING AROMA,
IS JUST THE RIGHT BEGINNING TO A PARTY. KEEP IT WARM
AND LADLE IT OUT OVER THE EVENING.

1 quart apple cider

2 star anise pods

1 cinnamon stick

4 whole cloves

1 whole nutmeg

2 black peppercorns

Put the apple cider in a large, nonreactive saucepan. Using a small muslin bag or a square made of double layers of cheesecloth, tie the remaining ingredients in a sachet. Put it in the cider and bring to a simmer over medium heat. Reduce heat to low and simmer for 20 minutes. Remove and discard the spice sachet. To serve, ladle into cups with handles. *Makes four 8-ounce servings*

# Sparkling Grapefruit and Raspberry Punch

THIS IS A SPARKLING, REFRESHING PUNCH THAT COMBINES THE SWEETNESS OF RASPBERRY WITH THE PIQUANCY OF GRAPEFRUIT.

2 cups grapefruit juice

2/3 cup raspberry syrup

2 tablespoons granulated sugar

2 quarts club soda

2 cups fresh raspberries

In a large bowl, combine the grapefruit juice, syrup, and sugar. Stir to dissolve the sugar. Add the club soda and stir again. Stir in the raspberries. *Makes about 3 quarts, or eighteen 4-ounce servings*

# Campari and Soda

Ice cubes

2 ounces Campari

2 ounces soda water, chilled

1 teaspoon fresh orange juice, strained

1 orange twist

Put several ice cubes in a tall glass. Pour the Campari over them, then add the soda water and orange juice and stir. Garnish with the orange twist. *Serves 1*

# Italian Fruit Soda

ITALIAN FRUIT SODAS ARE BEAUTIFUL TO LOOK AT AND REFRESHING TO DRINK. DOZENS OF DIFFERENT FLAVORS CAN BE PURCHASED AT GROCERY AND SPECIALTY FOOD STORES. FOR THE BEST FRUIT FLAVOR, LOOK FOR THOSE THAT ARE MADE WITH PURE FRUIT AND NATURAL INGREDIENTS.

2 ounces Italian fruit syrup, such as raspberry, mint, black currant, or orange

Ice cubes (optional)

6 ounces club soda or sparkling water, chilled

1 slice lemon or orange zest

Mint or tarragon sprig for garnish

Pour the fruit syrup into a tall glass, with or without ice. Add the club soda or sparkling water, twist the zest and add it, and stir to mix. Garnish with the sprig. *Makes one 8-ounce serving*

# Raspberry Vodka Martinis

MARTINIS ARE THE DRINK OF THE MOMENT, AND THERE
ARE PLENTY OF INTERESTING VARIATIONS ON THE CLASSIC
RECIPE, SUCH AS THIS ONE WITH A TANGY TASTE.

Ice cubes

3-1/2 ounces raspberry vodka

1/2 ounce dry vermouth

2 fresh raspberries

In an ice-filled shaker, combine the vodka and vermouth. Shake,
then strain into 2 martini glasses. Add a single raspberry to each.
*Serves 2*

# Fresh Fruit Spritzers

SPARKLING AND CRISP, FRUIT SPRITZERS MAKE
A FESTIVE DRINK FOR THE HOLIDAYS, ESPECIALLY WHEN
GARNISHED WITH SMALL FRESH OR FROZEN FRUITS.

4 ounces cranberry, apple, or other fruit juice

4 ounces club soda or sparkling water

1 teaspoon fresh lemon juice

Fresh raspberries, blackberries, or strawberries

Combine the juice and club soda in an 8-ounce glass. Stir in the
lemon juice and garnish with fresh fruit that has been frozen in ice
cubes. *Makes one 8-ounce serving*

# Blood Orange Champagne Cocktail

FEW DRINKS ARE MORE ELEGANT THAN A CHAMPAGNE COCKTAIL. WHEN MADE WITH ORANGE JUICE, AS THIS ONE IS,
IT IS OFTEN CALLED A MIMOSA. BLOOD ORANGE JUICE ADDS A DEEP COLOR TO THE DRINK.

1 ounce fresh blood orange juice, strained

3 ounces chilled Champagne

Dash of Angostura bitters

Pour the orange juice into a Champagne flute.

Add the Champagne and the bitters and stir. Serve immediately. *Serves 1*

# Metric Conversion Table

## LIQUID WEIGHTS

| U.S. Measurements | Metric Equivalents |
|---|---|
| 1/4 teaspoon | 1.23 ml |
| 1/2 teaspoon | 2.5 ml |
| 3/4 teaspoon | 3.7 ml |
| 1 teaspoon | 5 ml |
| 1 dessertspoon | 10 ml |
| 1 tablespoon (3 teaspoons) | 15 ml |
| 2 tablespoons (1 ounce) | 30 ml |
| 1/4 cup | 60 ml |
| 1/3 cup | 80 ml |
| 1/2 cup | 120 ml |
| 2/3 cup | 160 ml |
| 3/4 cup | 180 ml |
| 1 cup (8 ounces) | 240 ml |
| 2 cups (1 pint) | 480 ml |
| 3 cups | 720 ml |
| 4 cups (1 quart) | 1 liter |
| 4 quarts (1 gallon) | 3.8 liters |

## DRY WEIGHTS

| U.S. Measurements | Metric Equivalents |
|---|---|
| 1/4 ounce | 7 grams |
| 1/3 ounce | 10 grams |
| 1/2 ounce | 14 grams |
| 1 ounce | 28 grams |
| 1-1/2 ounces | 42 grams |
| 1-3/4 ounces | 50 grams |
| 2 ounces | 57 grams |
| 3-1/2 ounces | 100 grams |
| 4 ounces (1/4 pound) | 114 grams |
| 6 ounces | 170 grams |
| 8 ounces (1/2 pound) | 227 grams |
| 9 ounces | 250 grams |
| 16 ounces (1 pound) | 464 grams |

## TEMPERATURES

| Fahrenheit | Celsius (Centigrade) |
|---|---|
| 32°F (water freezes) | 0°C |
| 200°F | 95°C |
| 212°F (water boils) | 100°C |
| 250°F | 120°C |
| 275°F | 135°C |
| 300°F (slow oven) | 150°C |
| 325°F | 160°C |
| 350°F (moderate oven) | 175°C |
| 375°F | 190°C |
| 400°F (hot oven) | 205°C |
| 425°F | 220°C |
| 450°F (very hot oven) | 230°C |
| 475°F | 245°C |
| 500°F (extremely hot oven) | 260°C |

## LENGTH

| U.S. Measurements | Metric Equivalents |
|---|---|
| 1/8 inch | 3 mm |
| 1/4 inch | 6 mm |
| 3/8 inch | 1 cm |
| 1/2 inch | 1.2 cm |
| 3/4 inch | 2 cm |
| 1 inch | 2.5 cm |
| 1-1/4 inches | 3.1 cm |
| 1-1/2 inches | 3.7 cm |
| 2 inches | 5 cm |
| 3 inches | 7.5 cm |
| 4 inches | 10 cm |

## APPROXIMATE EQUIVALENTS

1 kilo is slightly more than 2 pounds.

1 liter is slightly more than 1 quart.

1 centimeter is approximately 3/8 inch.

# List of Recipes

# List of Crafts

# Index